This book belongs to:

Are you looking for a fun and relaxing way to de-stress and relax? Adult coloring books are the perfect way to do it! With so many intricate designs and patterns for coloring, this coloring book is sure to provide hours of enjoyment. Whether you are a beginner or a seasoned colorist, you are sure to find something to love in this book. So grab your favorite colored pencils or markers and get started!

This coloring book is filled with beautiful and detailed illustrations of animals from the jungle, including deer, monkeys, birds and more. With so many different animals to color in, this book is perfect for anyone who loves the jungle and wants to learn more about the animals that live there.